Ain't Nothing But A Man

My Quest To Find The Real John Henry

Scott Reynolds Nelson
With Marc Aronson

EasyRead Large

Copyright Page from the Original Book

PUBLISHED BY THE NATIONAL GEOGRAPHIC SOCIETY
John M. Fahey, Jr., **President and Chief Executive Officer**
Gilbert M. Grosvenor, **Chairman of the Board**
Nina D. Hoffman, **Executive Vice President; President, Book Publishing Group**

STAFF FOR THIS BOOK
Nancy Laties Feresten, **Vice President, Editor-in-Chief of Children's Books**
Bea Jackson, **Design and Illustrations Director, Children's Books**
Mary Beth Oelkers-Keegan, Jennifer Emmett, **Project Editors**
Lori Epstein, **Illustrations Editor**
Rebecca Baines, **Editorial Assistant**
Jennifer A. Thornton, **Managing Editor**
R. Gary Colbert, **Production Director**
Lewis R. Bassford, **Production Manager**
Maryclare Tracy, Nicole Elliott, **Manufacturing Managers**

A BOOK BY ARONSON & GLENN LLC
Produced by Marc Aronson and John W. Glenn
Book design, art direction, and production by Jon Glick, mouse+tiger

Copyright © 2008 by Scott Reynolds Nelson and Aronson & Glenn LLC

All rights reserved. Reproduction of the whole or any part of the contents without written permission from the National Geographic Society is strictly prohibited.

Library of Congress Cataloging-in-Publication Data

Nelson, Scott Reynolds.
Ain't nothing but a man : my quest to find the real John Henry / Scott Reynolds Nelson with Marc Aronson.
   p. cm.
Includes bibliographical references and index.
ISBN 978-1-4263-0000-4 (trade : alk. paper) — ISBN 978-1-4263-0001-1 (library alk. paper)
1. Henry, John William, 1847?–ca. 1875. 2. African Americans—Biography. 3. Railroad construction workers—United States—Biography. 4. John Henry (Legendary character) 5. Henry, John William, 1847?–ca. 1875—Homes and haunts. 6. Nelson, Scott Reynolds—Travel—Southern States. 7. Southern States—Description and travel. I. Aronson, Marc. II. Title.
E185.97.H4835N45 2008
975.03460730092—dc22
[B]

Illustration Credits
Abbreviations:
LOC = courtesy The Library of Congress
SRN = courtesy of Scott Reynolds Nelson
t = top, b = bottom, c = center, l = left, r = right

Front cover photograph of tracklayers courtesy SRN.
Jacket background, and illustration on front cover (t) and pages 1 and 3, reprinted with permission of Simon & Schuster Adult Publishing Group from *The Fireside Book of Folk Songs* by Margaret Bradford Boni, musical arrangements by Norman Lloyd; illustrations by Alice Provensen and Martin Provensen, copyright © 1947, and renewed © 1975, by Simon & Schuster, Inc. and Artists and Writers Guild, Inc. Endpapers illustration courtesy the estate of James Henry Daugherty. Tracklayer illustration above and on pages 7, 11, 15, 21, 29, 33, 42, 49, 55, and back cover: Aldren A. Watson, illustration from *John Henry and His Hammer* by Harold W. Felton. Copyright 1950 by Alfred A. Knopf, Inc. Reprinted with the permission of Aldren A. Watson c/o The Permissions Company, www.permissionscompany.com. All Rights Reserved.

Page 2: SRN; page 6: LOC; page 7: courtesy the estate of James Henry Daugherty; page 8: courtesy of the Hayden Family Revocable Art Trust; pages 10, 12-13, 14, 16, and 17 (b): SRN; page 17 (t): LOC; pages 18-19, 20, 22-23, and 24 (r): LOC; page 24 (l): SRN; page 25: LOC; pages 26-27: courtesy the Swem Library, College of William and Mary; pages 27 and 28: SRN; page 30: illustrations by Jon Glick, mouse+tiger; pages 32-33 (all): LOC; page 34: SRN; pages 36-37: LOC; page 39: courtesy of Douglas Owsley, Curator, Department of Anthropology, National Museum of Natural History, Smithsonian Institution, Washington, D.C.; page 40: courtesy the National Archives; pages 41, 42, 44, and 45: LOC; page 46: courtesy the Cook Collection, Valentine Richmond History Center; page 47: LOC; page 48: Frank W. Long's "John Henry" courtesy of Warren and Julie Payne, Payne Fine Arts, Louisville, Kentucky; pages 48, 50, and 55: SRN; page 54: courtesy the Swem Library, College of William and Mary; page 56: courtesy the Library of Virginia; page 60: LOC; page 60: map by Jon Glick, mouse+tiger.

Endpapers: The drawing of John Henry on the endpapers is by James Henry Daugherty, from his art for Irwin Shapiro's John Henry and the Double-Jointed Steam Drill, *published in 1933. In the book, the author matches the art with words suited to his retelling of the legend. The lyrics here are from a traditional version of the song itself. Page 2: A crew of railroad workers poses for the camera in 1911.*

Founded in 1888, the National Geographic Society is one of the largest nonprofit scientific and educational organizations in the world. It reaches more than 285 million people worldwide each month through its official journal, NATIONAL GEOGRAPHIC, and its four other magazines; the National Geographic Channel; television documentaries; radio programs; films; books; videos and DVDs; maps; and interactive media. National Geographic has funded more than 8,000 scientific research projects and supports an education program combating geographic illiteracy.

For more information, please call
1-800-NGS LINE (647-5463)
or write to the following address:

National Geographic Society
1145 17th Street N.W.
Washington, D.C. 20036-4688 U.S.A.

Visit us online at www.nationalgeographic.com/books

For information about special discounts for bulk purchases, please contact National Geographic Books Special Sales: ngspecsales@ngs.org

Printed in China.
12/RRDS/1

TABLE OF CONTENTS

CHAPTER ONE: STUCK	1
CHAPTER TWO: SCAVENGER	7
CHAPTER THREE: WHO WERE THE 40,000 MISSING MEN?	12
CHAPTER FOUR: FOLLOWING THE CLUES IN THE SONG ABOUT JOHN HENRY	21
CHAPTER FIVE: BIG BEND	32
CHAPTER SIX: BREAKTHROUGH	39
CHAPTER SEVEN: ON TRIAL	51
CHAPTER EIGHT: THE CONTEST	60
CHAPTER NINE: THE TRACKLINERS SPEAK	70
APPENDICES	77
SUGGESTIONS FOR FURTHER READING	91
A NOTE ABOUT MY SOURCES	97
BACK COVER MATERIAL	100
Index	103

i

To another John, John Nelson, who taught his sons that to understand something you have to take it apart, and to love something you need to put it back together again.
1938-2007

A locomotive like this pulled the first train to cross the Allegheny Mountains in 1873. How this locomotive came to roll through the hard rock of the mountains separating Virginia from the Ohio River is at the heart of this book's story.

CHAPTER ONE

STUCK

"This Hammer Going to Be the Death of Me"

October 1998: I was sitting at my desk at home, staring at the computer screen, stuck. I had promised to give a talk about some historical research I was doing on men who worked on the railroad, but I couldn't figure out what to say. My wall was filled with books, my desktop covered with letters, schoolwork, more books, computer games, Post-its. Stacked beneath the table were boxes piled high with photocopies of documents. I had a book open on my lap. I had scanned an old postcard from the period I was studying to be the background of my computer monitor. I was surrounded with research, and I did not know what to write.

John Henry as drawn by James Daugherty in a book for children published in 1945.

John Henry lies dead after beating the steam drill in this painting by the African-American painter Palmer C. Hayden. Born in 1890, Hayden grew up in Virginia where his father sang John Henry songs to him. In the 1940s, Hayden used his memories of the men he grew up with to craft a series of paintings about John Henry.

For years I had been following a trail, and it was stone cold. I wanted to know if there was a real John Henry, the man in the song who was so strong he beat a steam drill in a contest, but then laid down his hammer and died:

When John Henry was a little bitty baby

*No bigger than the palm of your hand
His daddy looked down at Johnnie and said
Johnnie's going to be a steel driving man
Lawd, Lawdy
Johnnie's going to be a steel driving man*

*When John Henry was a little bitty baby
Sitting on his daddy's knee
Well, he picked up a hammer and a little piece of steel
He said this hammer's going to be the death of me
Lawd, Lawdy
This hammer's going to be the death of me!*

I had listened to hundreds of versions of the song and visited all the places that seemed linked to John Henry. I had read books about him by other historians. But nothing made sense, nothing added up. Maybe he was just a myth, an invention, no more real than Paul Bunyan.

I was sitting at my computer, cruising, trawling for anything that might come my way. And then as I stared at the scanned postcard I had seen a thousand times before, I suddenly saw it, the clue that changed everything.

The photo has the quality of a still from a movie, as if it were filmed from a moving train. It shows railway workers "making the grade" along a stretch of track in the South in the 1870s. To make the grade, teams of men dug up dirt and rocks and moved them around to make sure that the slope of the rail bed was smooth and even.

CHAPTER TWO

SCAVENGER

"And every locomotive come roarin' by"

To explain what that card told me, I have to begin long before I ever saw it. I did not start out looking for John Henry. In fact that search was part of a larger mystery I was trying to solve. But that is the way I work: I am a historian, and my work is an endless scavenger hunt. No matter what assignment I am working on, I keep picking up clues and filing them away. I often don't know when I will use those bits of information, but I have them, and sometimes they come in handy. So let me take you through the trail as I followed it, until it led me back to the postcard on my screen, and to finding the real John Henry.

Ever since I was a boy, I have loved looking for strange old things. Growing up in Florida, my dad and two younger brothers and I would put on thick boots and hunt through dumpsters, or go out on backroads, to look for cool finds. Our best discovery was the curved hood of an old car, which made a great sled when my dad pulled it with his car. But anything was interesting to us. When we found a chair, an old matchbox toy, a battered pot, we examined each one as a clue in a detective story. Holding a piece of the past, we competed to imagine how the people who used it dressed, what they cooked, why they broke this chair. We also found clues to the past without ever having to leave home.

All over the South you see the paths of railroads—some with loaded cars passing every day, some abandoned. As a child in Sanford, Florida, I lived near the very last stop of the auto-train—the train line where passengers could ship their cars with them. The tracks passed through a patch of woods and vines—potato vines we called them, because they had fruits on them that look like potatoes and were the perfect size and weight to use as ammunition in fights. The woods, the vines, and the tracks gave us a hideout, a place to play, and many chances to imagine life on the railroad.

Taken around 1912, this photo shows a crew of southern railroad workers on the job. Road crews were often led by a white boss—in this case, probably the man in the center standing on the wagon and leaning on the long board. I began researching the song "John Henry" as a way to learn more about African-American workers such as these men.

When I reached college, and then graduate school, I decided to combine my impulse to follow up on historical clues with my interest in railroads. In fact, I spent years studying the railroads of the South. Studying history may seem to be about filling up with knowledge—like a car pulling into a gas station. Once you have a full tank, you are done. But it is just the opposite. The more you know about the past, the more questions you ask. Once you have a handle on what others have found, you can see the gaps, the spaces, the places that have not been covered. This is exactly what happened to me, for even before I ever thought about John Henry, I discovered that some 40,000 men, the largest railroad workforce in the South, were hardly mentioned in the history books. Why? I set out to learn more about those men. That was the big mystery I was trying to solve.

Track workers pose on a handcar in 1911. Railroad work was hard and dangerous, but railroad men flocked to the jobs because they were paid in cash, often weekly.

CHAPTER THREE

WHO WERE THE 40,000 MISSING MEN?

"I can line a track"

At a glance, railroad tracks seem to be one long ribbon of steel. But in fact track is laid down in short segments that every train jostles as it passes by. In order for trains to run smoothly, the sections of track must be constantly aligned and realigned. Rocks and gravel that protect track beds must be refilled and maintained. Today a machine takes care of much of the track alignment, but in the 19th century, it was the done by crews of trackliners.

Day after day, a line boss would go out in an inspection car to check for places where tracks needed work. Anytime he saw a problem, he would throw a red handkerchief out of the window and onto the nearby ground. Then a crew of men watched over by a walking boss would fix the track. Out West, trackliners were either Irish or Chinese. No one ever counted the track liners, but a company usually had one man for every mile of track, and there were 40,000 miles of track in the South. So it is safe to say that about 40,000 trackliners, most African-American, worked throughout the South.

    I wanted to know more about these men and the lives they led. But they cannot be found in history books, and few of the black workers, especially just after the Civil War, knew how to write. All I could do was to keep my eye open for any source that might tell me more about them. One day in a library I found a set of letters that the archive had gathered only by mistake. The writer had the same name as a well-known southern journalist, so the library assumed they were important documents. Instead they were almost unreadable notes jotted down with a purple crayon by Henry Grady, a white railroad carpenter who worked all over the South between 1882 and 1888. Grady's scrawled letters to his sister described track workers sleeping in railroad cars and mangled in terrible accidents. His letters were like a fuzzy picture—they gave me a glimpse of the trackliners, but only through his eyes.

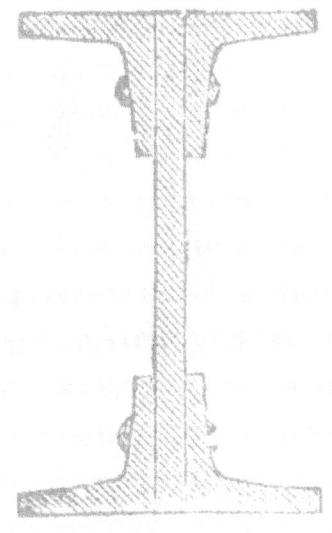

New rails would beheld in place by the overhanging heads of long iron spikes, hammered down into the wooden ties on either side of the flat-bottomed rails. If you look closely at the left-hand track in the photograph, you can see the flat heads of the spikes lining the edges of the rail.

Once upon a time, historians were trained to spend all their time poring over official documents and other writings left from the past. But more recently they have realized that the past comes down to us in many ways. Some scholars study fashions, others foods. Some sit in graveyards looking at the decorations on tombstones, and more and more historians pay attention to songs.

You cannot always trust the words of a song—there is no reason to believe that there was a real farmer who had a dog named Bingo or that anyone actually believed there was a mountain made out of rock candy. Yet sometimes there are clues in a song that historians can trace: Many scholars believe that "ashes, ashes, all fall down" from "Ring Around the Rosy" is telling the story of the Black Plague in London, where so many people died. Trackliners were known to sing while they worked. I asked myself two questions—how can you tell which songs the trackliners sang? And what do the songs tell us?

"Dogging the track": Here a two-man team aligns track just the way larger crews of trackliners did in the South. This photo was taken near Anchorage, Alaska, sometime between 1900 and 1916.

Work songs of all kinds are more about rhythm than words or melody. In order to march in step, an army unit or marching band will count out: "I **left** my wife and **48** kids; **Left** (pause), **left** (pause), **left** right, **left**." Sailors on ships sang shanties paced to help them hoist sails. As gangs of slaves picked cotton, they sang

> ***Jump*** *down,* ***turn*** *around,*
> ***Pick*** *a bale of* ***cot*** *ton,*
> ***Jump*** *down,* ***turn*** *around,*
> ***Pick*** *a bale a* ***day,***
>
> ***Jump*** *down,* ***turn*** *around,*
> ***Pick*** *a bale of* ***cot*** *ton,*
> ***Jump*** *down,* ***turn*** *around,*
> ***Pick*** *a bale a* ***day***
>
> ***Oh*** *Lordy,* ***pick*** *a bale of cotton,*
> ***Oh*** *Lordy,* ***pick*** *a bale a day,*
> ***Oh*** *Lordy,* ***pick*** *a bale of cotton,*
> ***Oh*** *Lordy,* ***pick*** *a bale a day.*

To move track you first have to lift it—pushing the heavy steel up when it has been hammered down as hard as possible. The only way to get that bar to move is to have the whole team press down together. Each man carried a tool called a "dog." If a song was paced right, every man in the team would dog the track at the same moment. (See photo above.) So tracklining songs needed to leave a space, just the right space, for the sound of the men pushing down on their dogs, moving the track.

The song about John Henry and his hammer comes in countless versions. When railroad workers who did not need a work rhythm sang the song, they made it into a ballad. It had many, many verses, some taken from other songs. "John Henry" was like a long story that you could spin out, adding verses all the livelong day. But the version sung by trackliners is different. Their song is much more bare bones, with a beat so clear you can't miss it:

The world of railroad work—the drilling, digging, and hammering, the endless toil of shifting rails—is the subject of this 1936 print by artist Manuel Silberger. Many artists at that time set out to honor working people.

Take this hammer, **huh**
Give it to the captain, **huh**
Tell him I'm gone, **huh**
Tell him I'm gone, **huh**

I decided to use the song of John Henry as a piece of evidence, a way to learn more about trackliners. In the song, John Henry is a man who drills into rock, not a trackliner. So the song would not tell me about them directly. And if he were a myth, the song would only tell me about the trackliners' dreams and hopes, not their experiences. So I needed to get to know everything I could about the song and to see if it led to a real person.

Then I might learn more about these silent and missing men.

The fundamentals of tracklining are on display in this illustration from 1881. Steel rails are laid over heavy wooden ties, and then iron spikes are hammered down on either side to hold the rails in place.

CHAPTER FOUR

FOLLOWING THE CLUES IN THE SONG ABOUT JOHN HENRY

"He's the best steel-driver on the C&O Road"

There are hundreds of versions of the song about John Henry. Some of them contain very specific information. For example,

> When John Henry was a little lad
> A-holding of his papa's hand,
> Says "If I live until I'm twenty-one,
> I'm goin' to make a steel-driving man."

> And Johnny said, when he was a man
> He made his words come true,

*He's the best steel-driver on the C&O Road,
He belongs to the steel-driving crew.*

If there was a real John Henry, he could have worked for the C&O—the Covington & Ohio Railroad (which later became known as the Chesapeake & Ohio Railway). But other versions took the story in completely different directions.

*John Henry had a little woman
Well her name was Polly Ann
Well John Henry took sick and he had to go to bed
Well and Polly drove steel like a man (well, well)
Well and Polly drove steel like a man*

*Well they's some said he come from England
Well they's some said he come from Spain (a yah)
Well but I say he musta been a West Virginia man
Cause he died with the hammer in his hand (my lord)*

Well he died with the hammer in his hand

Like the message in a big game of telephone, the song kept changing as it was passed from one person to another. I knew that I would have to follow all these leads to understand what each version of the song could tell us. But I started with the clues about John Henry himself that others had already found in the song.

A construction train on the Union Pacific Railroad, ca 1860-65. By 1869, train tracks linked the East and West coasts. The great success of uniting the nation by train encouraged businessmen to tackle the challenge of blasting through the hard rock of the Allegheny Mountains.

People who had studied the song before me decided that John Henry had indeed worked for the C&O and had held a contest with a steam drill. Some versions even said where that battle was held:

When John Henry was a little boy,
He was sitting on his mama's knee;
Says, "The Big Bend Tunnel on the C and O road
Is going to be the death of me, Lord, Lord,
Is going to be the death of me."

> ## THE PACIFIC COAST.
>
> ### THE NITRO-GLYCERINE EXPLOSION IN SAN FRANCISCO.
>
> Terrific Effects of the New Explosive Compound—Horrible Scene—Entire Demolition of the Building—Melancholy Loss of Life—Minute Description of the Tragic Event.
>
> From Our Own Correspondent.
>
> SAN FRANCISCO, Tuesday, April 17, 1866.
>
> "From sudden death, good Lord deliver us!" Never until now was I impressed with the significance and import of the above supplication.

The New York Times of April 17, 1866, describes the "horrible scene" when nitroglycerine accidentally exploded. Still, Collis Potter Huntington was absolutely certain of the railroad-building power of nitroglycerine and new steam drills.

Luckily, I already knew something about the C&O. Collis Huntington, the owner of the company, was a famous railroad man. In fact, he was one of the four men behind laying the track that linked the coasts of America by rail—which was celebrated in the Golden Spike ceremony on May 10, 1869.

Huntington learned a great deal in that scramble to put tracks where nature did not want them. His men used new forms of explosives such as dynamite (which is portable nitroglycerine) as soon as they were developed. Powerful controlled explosions allowed crews of Chinese laborers to blast tunnels through the Sierra Mountains instead of having to go over or around them. Huntington also heard that a new kind of drill had been invented, powered by steam. There were two versions of this wonder, and one was even tipped with diamond points. A steam drill could make fast, regular holes in the hardest rock, and then a pour of nitroglycerine or sticks of dynamite placed in those gaps would shatter the surrounding stone. Teams of men with drills and explosives could march through any mountain like a hungry animal devouring meat.

THE GOLDEN SPIKE AND THE TRANSCONTINENTAL RAILROAD

On May 10, 1869, America changed. On that date, at Promontory Point, Utah, the last spike was driven into the track joining the Union Pacific and Central Pacific railroad lines, as shown in the illustration above from 1869. Some 2,000 miles of the country were now connected by rail. Trips from the East to the West that were once measured in months now took days. Four

businessmen, Leland Stanford, Collis Huntington, Charles Crocker, and Mark Hopkins, are usually credited with completing the railroads through the western mountains. But it was only possible because of the dangerous labor of the Chinese and Irish workmen who blasted their way through the Sierras and lay the track across the desert. The actual ceremony involved hammering a spike made of gold, and news of the great event was immediately telegraphed around the nation.

Huntington was so confident he made a bet. In 1866 he promised the government of Virginia that he could build a line linking eastern Virginia to the Ohio River within six years, by 1872. If he could do that, he wagered, the line would belong to him. If he failed, he would give every inch of track to the state. Huntington's rivals must have smiled. They knew that to win the bet he would have to find a way through the Allegheny Mountain range, which has some of the hardest rock in the world. He probably smiled too, because of what he knew about dynamite and had heard about the new steam drills.

Percussive steam drill, ca 1860s. This elaborate mechanism was rolled into place on a carriage and was used to drill both horizontally and vertically through rock. The tubes at left and in the middle supplied power to as many as five drills, which punched or pounded the rock face.

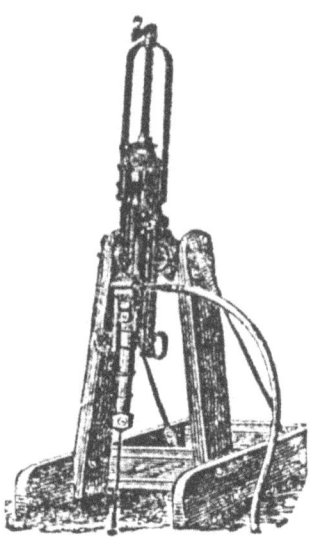

Burleigh drill, 1871. Charles Burleigh was a steam engine builder who made some of the first successful percussive drills in the 1860s and 1870s. His drills were so widely used that steam drills were often referred to as Burleigh drills.

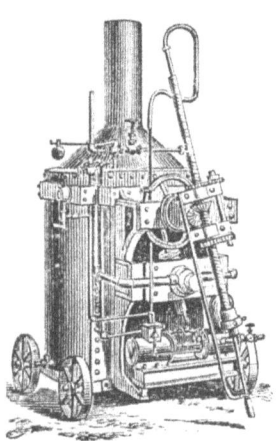

Leschot's rotary diamond drill, 1870. A competitor to percussive drills, diamond drills used steam pressure to turn a drill tipped with cheap black diamonds. They worked best on softer rock and were almost always used for drilling down, rather than across.

Big Bend (or Great Bend) Tunnel, 2002.

CHAPTER FIVE

BIG BEND

"The Big Bend Tunnel on the C and O road"

If John Henry really existed, then maybe it was at Big Bend that he hammered steel in a contest against Huntington's steam drills. The Big Bend Tunnel (sometimes called the Great Bend) is not hard to find; it is on maps of West Virginia. There is even a statue of John Henry in a town near the tunnel. If I was going to learn anything more about John Henry, I had to go to Big Bend and see the tunnel for myself.

To understand how a tunnel was built, you have to look at it from all sides. Big Bend Tunnel is no longer used, and the entrance had once been sealed with boulders. But now you can walk right into it. As I explored, what

I was seeing did not make sense. John Henry is a hero in the song because he could drill farther into hard rock than the steam drill. But I knew enough geology to see that the red rock in Big Bend Tunnel was not particularly hard. Though the rock is called "hard red shale," it crumbles when exposed to air, and it is so soft that the tunnel suffered a cave-in shortly after it was built.

My father had shown me that following backroads, what are called "junk" roads, often leads to the best finds. So when I saw a neglected old side road running up Big Bend Mountain, I had to explore it. I knew that even as men pushed their way through the mountain, another team must have dug from the top down. They were creating pathways so that buckets filled with rock could be hauled out. The road led me to the crest of the mountains, where I found traces of those top-down passages. Men working with steam drills needed a space at least 10 feet by 10 feet to operate. What I saw confirmed the hunch I'd had in the tunnel: Not one of those shafts was large enough to hold a steam drill; every one must have been made by hand.

> ## HOW STEAM DRILLS WERE USED IN TUNNELING THROUGH MOUNTAINS
>
> **Railroad engineers in the 1800s often attacked a mountain from more than one angle, hoping to find the places where it was easiest to drill. While some men drilled straight into the mountainside to carve out the main tunnel, others drilled down from the top of the mountain to create a vertical shaft that would connect with the main tunnel. This shaft allowed fresh air into the main tunnel and was also used to clear the loose rock thrown off by the drillers working across the mountain. Rocks chipped away by the steam drills would be gathered up and lifted out by a system of ropes and buckets. Many of the steam drills used to drill through mountains were percussive steam drills, which used the force of**

steam pressure to drive a drill bit into rock. The illustration below is based on actual drawings from when the C&O was blasting through mountains in what is now West Virginia.

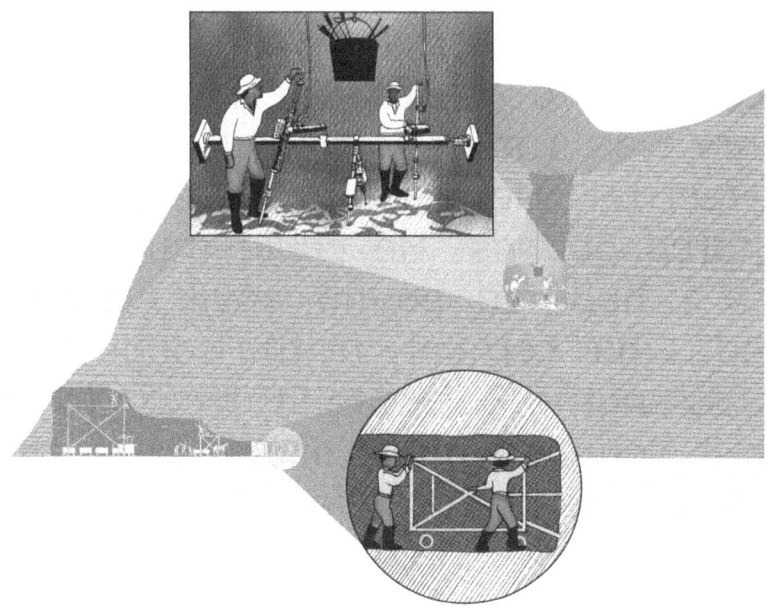

No steam drills were used making Big Bend Tunnel—I could see that with my own eyes. Nor was there any reason to pit man against machine to cut through that soft rock. I was sure that John Henry did not die here. But I had no idea where to look next. The song that I hoped would tell me more about the silent trackliners was a dead end.

I tried another approach, going back over the work of previous researchers, looking at their sources. Following that route, I found some letters from a man who claimed he had heard about John Henry from an old railroad worker who knew the steel-driving man personally. According to Leon R. Harris, "John Henry was a mighty man. He was over six feet tall. He weighed more than two hundred pounds. He could muscle and toss a hundred pound anvil with one hand." That certainly fit the songs about his strength. But was it true? To my ear it sounded more like a fable than a fact. Like the Big Bend Tunnel, Harris's story looked promising but did not give me any new answers.

But, as I said, I am a scavenger. I knew that when you set out to do historical research, you don't always know what you are looking for or what you will find. You just go on gathering interesting information related to the subject you are researching and keep your eyes open for what comes your way. While I worked on other projects,

I kept looking at versions of the song, trying to find more clues.

The changing landscape of the South: Before the work of the trackliners could begin, gangs of road workers needed to prepare level roadbeds such as this (photographed around 1900). The "shanties" that housed black railroad workers were similar to this long since demolished slave cabin (inset).

I gathered every scrap of evidence I could find about Virginia just after the Civil War. This was the very beginning of the period that textbooks call Reconstruction, when the government in Washington made an effort to protect newly freed slaves and whites in the South tried to regain as much control as they could. That gave me a sense of the tensions in the world of John Henry's time. I looked at photos that showed me black men in the South working on the railroad. I learned that those workers often lived in shacks built out of leftover cheap wood called "shantlings" so that the houses came to be known as "shanties." I cruised around the Internet to find something, anything more. I even promised to write a paper about trackliners' songs where I planned to talk about John Henry. But I was stuck.

The postcard from 1910 that I used as my desktop wallpaper.

CHAPTER SIX

BREAKTHROUGH

"There lays that steel drivin' man"

October 1998: I was listening to so many versions of John Henry that it was bothering my family—it was as if John Henry were driving steel in our own home. One afternoon I was working on my paper and thinking about the songs. I had a book by another historian who studied John Henry open and on my lap. And one verse kept coming into my mind:

They took John Henry to the white house,
And buried him in the san'
And every locomotive come roarin' by,
Says there lays that steel drivin' man,

Says there lays that steel drivin' man.

I looked up at my screen, where I had saved the postcard shown above. The image had become a background blur to me; I hardly paid attention to it. And then I saw it, and I finally understood the picture that unlocked the secret of John Henry:

The picture was an illustrated postcard showing the old buildings of the Virginia Penitentiary in Richmond. Most of the buildings were tinted red, suggesting the color of brick. One, though, blazed white. And running by the prison were train tracks.

A southern chain gang, ca 1884-91. The Virginia Penitentiary rented out convicts to the C&O

Railroad for 25 cents a day—one-fourth the going rate for free laborers.

What was the white house in the song? The president's home in Washington is the most famous White House—but it was not called that until 1901, well after these verses about John Henry were first sung. The picture was saying that John Henry was a prisoner. "No," I said out loud. I could not believe it. I felt chills running through my body, as if I'd seen a ghost.

Now I had a whole new set of questions. If I was right, and the song was talking about the Virginia Penitentiary, why was John Henry in prison? Why would he have been buried in the sand? And how did that connect to the C&O and steam drills and a contest of man against machine? Every question I asked led to more questions. And then I remembered something I had seen in Henry Grady's letters: Grady noticed that "several hundred state convicts" were used to work on the railroad. If convicts were employed in Louisiana, could that also have been true in Virginia?

One of my other scavenging finds answered my own question. Years earlier I had come across a report issued by the Board of the Virginia Penitentiary in 1872. They were concerned because so many of the prisoners who had been hired out to work on the railroad were dying.

As I pieced together all of these bits of evidence, I realized that I had one more clue that related directly to the song. Six months earlier a historian at the Museum of the Confederacy had told me about a strange discovery. As a contractor took down the old Virginia Penitentiary buildings he found some 300 skeletons. The archaeologist who was called in to study the bones concluded that they were probably African-American and from around the late 1800s.

The men had been buried with the kind of small objects prisoners might keep with them in their cells: A small piece of granite, a penny cut into quarters, an old vulcanized rubber comb melted down and turned into a ring.

The bodies of prisoners from the penitentiary were hidden on the grounds, buried in the rock, mud, and gravel of the gully. Layers of sand separated the boxes holding the skeletons and the small objects. No gravestones marked the burials. If it were not for a modern contractor's shovel, no would know that underneath the gully next to the prison lay the skeletons of 300 men. As the song said,

> *They took John Henry to the white house,*
> *And buried him in the san'*

The tracks of the Richmond, Fredericksburg & Potomac railroad passed right by the gully hiding the skeletons of the men. Again, that is just what the song said:

> *And every locomotive come roarin' by,*
> *Says there lays that steel drivin' man,*
> *Says there lays that steel drivin' man.*

The song lyric, Grady's letter, the report to the prison board, the 300 skeletons: All of the pieces of evidence linked together. One of the strangest lyrics in John Henry was turning out to be simple truth. Did that mean the rest of the song was true?

Prisons keep records. They need to list who is there, for how long, and why. I needed to find those documents, for that would allow me to test the theory about the white house. But now I faced a new roadblock. It was not hard to find out that the records were housed at the Library of Virginia; I learned that when I began my research. But I was told the papers were not available to the public. This was worse than being stuck after visiting Big Bend. Then, I didn't know whether I would ever find a new lead. Now I knew exactly what I wanted and where it was—but I faced a stone wall.

Taken in 1992 when they were discovered, this photo show the remains of two African-American men found buried in coffins on the grounds of the Virginia Penitentiary.

I use that library often, for many different projects. So now, month after month, for four long years, every time I arrived there, I asked to be allowed to see the records. The answer was always no. There is very little a researcher can do when an archivist says that a file is closed. There may be any number of reasons: The papers could be damaged and being preserved, the documents could be too fragile to touch, or the library may prefer to put them in order before turning them over to scholars. In the manuscript room of the library, the holdings are kept behind metal gates. When, and if, they ever unlock those doors is up to them. All you can do is to keep asking.

I became even more eager to see the records in 2002 when I found a census report, which listed "John William Henry" as being a prisoner in the Virginia Penitentiary. I simply had to see that prison record. Finally, yet another a year later, a librarian I had never met before was seated at the reference desk. I asked her about the prison records—I just didn't mention the many previous times I'd asked and been denied.

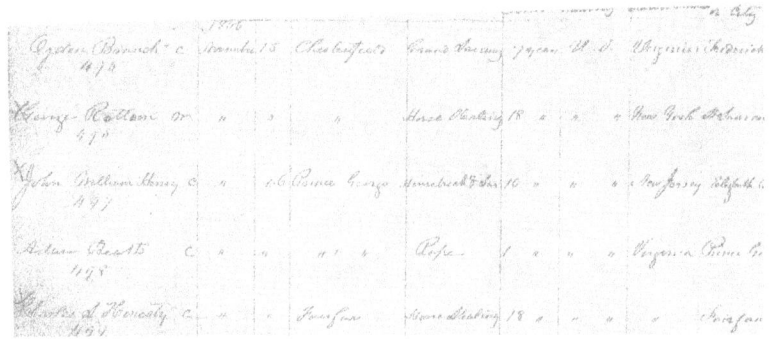

An 1870 census report listed a "John William Henry" as a prisoner in the Virginia Penitentiary. Seeing this made me redouble my efforts to study the prison records.

After looking at the papers on her desk, she saw that the records were closed but didn't know of any reason why they should be. She said something like, "after all it's public record who gets put into the penitentiary"—which is true. She took out a pencil, crossed out "closed" on the listing, and pointed me to the manuscripts room. Then she called them to say it was fine, they should give me the records.

When I opened the boxes I could see why the library had kept the records sealed: they had not been sorted at all. The big ledger dated "1865-1870s" that recorded prisoners admitted into the jail was two feet high and almost a foot wide. The rest of the records in the box were covered with something black that looked like coal dust—I suspect that the files had been stored near a coal furnace. Soon my arms and cheeks were coated with a black dust that stung when I accidentally rubbed my eyes.

When you finally have a record in your hands that you have been after for years, you go very slowly because at any moment you might see something really important. Your heart is racing, but time slows down. Looking through the big ledger I found:

Virginia Penitentiary in 1865, the year before John William Henry arrived. Notice the large white building.

John William Henry c[olored] (#497)
WHEN RECEIVED: 1866 Nov.16
WHERE SENTENCED: Prince George
CRIME: Housebreak & larceny
TERM: 10 years
NATIVITY: US
STATE OR PROVINCE: New Jersey
COUNTY DIST OR CITY: Elizabeth City
HEIGHT: 5ft 1 1/4
AGE: 19
COMPLEXION: Black

COL OF HAIR: Black
COL OF EYES: Black
MARKS OR OTHER PECULIAR DESCRIPTIONS: a small scar on left arm above elbow. A small one on right arm above wrist.
WHEN PENSIONED, DISCHARGED, OR DIED: Transferred [in pencil]

My hands were shaking.

John William Henry had indeed been held in the Virginia Penitentiary where the bones of black men were buried in the sand. But how come he had been convicted of breaking into a home and stealing? To answer that I had to shift my focus from trying to pry the prison records out of the library to tracking down old trials in nearby courts. That trail was easier to follow.

John Henry, a worker in the headquarters of the 3rd Army Corps, in 1863. I would like to think that this was the John Henry later arrested in Prince George County, but we may never know.

CHAPTER SEVEN

ON TRIAL

"John Henry said to his Captain, 'A man ain't nothin' but a man'"

During the Civil War, the Union Army under General Grant had faced off against the Confederates just outside of Petersburg, Virginia. Protected by 40 miles of trenches and embankments, the southern soldiers held off the Union for two years—and when they gave in, in 1865, the war was over. Grant's headquarters during the long siege was eight miles behind the lines, at City Point, where two rivers met and a train line ended. This was the perfect supply depot for his army.

Right after the war, City Point became an instant city, an instant city filled with free black men. The Union Army paid its soldiers but left it up to them to find their way home. Black soldiers who no longer needed to fight, black cooks, and suppliers who been employed by the Union enjoyed the run of the town. The photo opposite of a man identified as John Henry shows one such man who had worked for the army. He is the right height to match the John Henry in the prison record, but that is all we know about him.

White people in Petersburg had just lost a terrible war. And they were not pleased to see so many free black men in their midst. The local paper complained that the black soldiers "strut through this improvised town with an evident air of satisfaction." You can almost hear the writer gnashing his teeth. Just at this moment, in a town where local whites hated seeing confident black men, John William Henry was arrested. "Prince George" listed in the prison record was the county in which City Point was located.

When I located the records of the court case, I learned that John Henry was taken in on April 26, 1866. We will never know if he really did steal any money at all from Wiseman's grocery store. One part of the case against him made little sense: He was accused of taking much more money than the store actually had—though it is just possible that the store owner lived upstairs, and a thief could have robbed him too. Even at the time, some people found the trial disturbing. A federal official who came to make sure the trial was fair wrote that "John W. Henry, a freed boy, was found guilty of having committed burglary, and sentenced to the penitentiary for ten years. The sentence seems a long one." It was long—the very most the law allowed.

The wharves of City Point, Prince George County, Virginia, in 1864. This photograph was taken at the time of the Union siege of nearby Petersburg.

A chain gang at work in Richmond, Virginia, from an illustration that ran in Harper's Weekly in 1868.

One way for local whites to take the strut out of a black man's step was to put him in prison. In fact, the penitentiary was filling up with black men. In October 1866 there were three black prisoners for every two whites. By January of 1867, there were 10 blacks for every white. Southerners who had just lost a war managed to convince courts to put hundreds of black men in prison, including black soldiers.

RECONSTRUCTION

This photo shows the first integrated jury in the South, gathered to judge Jefferson Davis, the president of the Confederacy. (The man highlighted at left is Burnham Wardwell, who became warden of Virginia Penitentiary in 1868.) From the moment that Abraham Lincoln issued the

Emancipation Proclamation, one key question was how the rest of the country would judge the slaveholding South. Former slaves were eager to marry, move away from the plantations, own their own farms. They wanted to learn, to vote, and to hold office. Former slave owners were determined to hold on to their workers, and feared their vengeance. The effort to rebuild the South in a way that protected blacks was called Reconstruction, and it lasted from 1863 to 1877. But Americans were not sure how to change race relations in the South, or even if that was a good idea. So the laws issued from Washington varied over time, and were not always enforced. Blacks in the South really only began to be treated as full citizens a century later, when the Civil Rights movement finally broke the back of segregation.

A southern chain gang in 1898. Prison work gangs, chained together and often wearing distinctive prison-issued uniforms, were a familiar part of the southern landscape after the Civil War.

Conditions in the prison were terrible: The cells were filthy, there were not enough beds so men had to double up, and the blankets were so filled with lice that a visitor suggested burning them up in a bonfire. But in 1868 a new warden came to take over the prison and improve the conditions. Burnham Wardwell meant well: He proposed ending punishments he found barbaric, such as gagging the prisoners.

But he made things worse, much worse, for John Henry.

Wardwell thought prisoners would do better out in the open air, so he agreed to rent them out as workers. One company was eager to take up the offer: the C&O, which had just four years left to cut through the Alleghenies. In the big ledger that the library finally let me see, I learned that on December 1, 1868, 15 prisoners left Richmond to work for the C&O. One of them was named John Henry.

Frank W. Long lived in Berea, Kentucky, in the 1930s and heard stories about John Henry from the white miners there. Still, he imagined John Henry as this powerful black man.

CHAPTER EIGHT

THE CONTEST

"I will beat that steam drill down"

Huntington's plan to use steam drills was not going well, as the new machines kept breaking down. In order to win his bet, he needed men to make the holes in the rock to hold explosives. The prisoners rented out to the C&O would have started out as "muckers," men who pulled the heavy rocks out of the blasted holes. But with time some learned to be "drillers," part of the crew that hammered those holes in the rock. While one man raised his hammer, another had to ready a drill bit in just the right spot. The hammer teams used songs to keep them in rhythm. The man who held the drill was called a shaker. Holding the drill bit between his legs, he would "rock" the chisel so it grabbed on to the best spot in the stone, or he would "roll" it to clear away broken chunks. Deep in the tunnels of the South, the term "rock and roll" was invented.

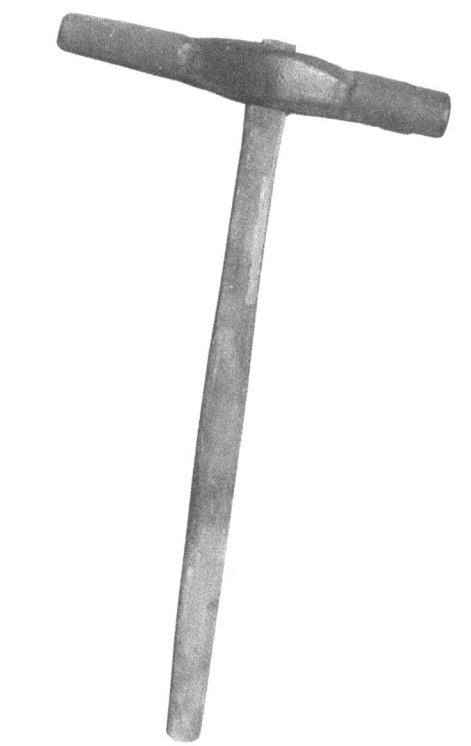

A 10-pound trackliner's hammer.

The big prison ledger had given me more that just a description of John Henry, for it mentioned where he and the other prisoners were sent to work: the Lewis Tunnel. Why? Why did the C&O need convicts to work at that particular tunnel? When I saw the white house postcard, I was stopped by the library that would not release the records of the prison. Now I faced a new problem. The detailed engineering reports of the C&O were missing. Those reports would tell me what kind of work went on in each C&O project. Rumor had it the reports had been burned up in a fire. Once again I was close, but stuck.

I took this shot of the Lewis Tunnel as I neared it in my car in 2003.

Historians learn that if one search through a library catalog does not work, you can try another. Computers are very fast, but they are very dumb, for they answer exactly the question you asked, not the question you meant to ask. For example, if you are looking for information on Benjamin Franklin, it might be listed under Ben Franklin, B. Franklin, or Franklin, B. Even though I could not find the report, I wondered if there was any information on the contractors—the engineers and crew bosses—who actually hired John Henry and the other prisoners. Once I found those names, I would search through library catalogs for information on them.

Sifting through versions of the song, old interviews with black workers, and other papers, I kept running into the name C.R. Mason. In one document he was even named as the man who supervised John Henry. But there was a problem: Previous historians had decided that Mason could not have worked with John Henry. Why? Because Mason had not worked at Big Bend. That didn't bother me. I had already concluded John Henry hadn't been to Big Bend either. But because those writers believed Big Bend was where John Henry died, they ignored the clues pointing to Mason.

Checking on Mason led me to the men he worked with: Tommy Walters, H.D. Whitcomb, A.H. Perry. If I could find any of their records, I had a chance of learning more about John Henry and the Lewis Tunnel.

I began hunting through every library collection I could find, looking for anything about those men. And then, just as with the postcard, I struck gold. A search engine called Worldcat allows you to search library collections all over the world. Looking under the contractors' names, I was directed to a historical society in Cleveland, Ohio, that actually had the missing engineering reports. Years ago an employee had brought them with him. Since it was not clear that he actually had the right to take the papers to the library, they had disappeared from sight. Only very recently had the library listed any information about the reports, but only by the names of the contractors, not by the titles of the documents. The only way to find the reports was by searching for the contractors—which I just happened to be doing.

The engineering reports confirmed what I had seen at the Big Bend Tunnel—no steam drills were needed to cut through the soft rock. That was fortunate for the C&O because the drills were failing. The engineers wanted to give them one final and fair test—to see if they could be used at all. Where should that be? While men with hammers worked on Big Bend, the C&O was also blasting another tunnel through much harder stone.

The engineering reports stated clearly that steam drills and men were tested against each other, and I learned exactly where: the Lewis Tunnel. I even knew when the test began: in August of 1870. But who were the men who hammered against the drills? The prison ledger mentioned that convicts were sent to that very tunnel. What work were they doing? The railroad was so proud of the labor in the tunnels that they invited newspaper reporters to come to the Lewis dig. One wrote that "a large body of men, mostly convicts from the State penitentiary, were at work in the various shafts and at both ends of the tunnel."

The reports were a treasure trove of information. When I put those reports together with the songs, I felt I finally could understand where and how John Henry died. Just as the song describes the prison, it also allows us to see exactly what happened in the contest:

The steam drill set on the right hand side,
John Henry was on the left.
He said, "I will beat that steam drill down
Or hammer my fool self to death."

The men that made that steam drill,
Thought it was mighty fine;
John Henry sunk a fourteen-foot hole
And the steam drill only made nine.

Lewis Tunnel, 2003. Between 1930 and 1932, the tunnel was widened and the front arch put in, as indicated by the inscription above the entrance.

I knew that when the men tunneled across the mountain, holes only went five feet into the rock at a time. But when the men dug down from the top of the mountain, they had to go 10 feet for each blast. The steam drill couldn't get there; John Henry went four feet past the line.

Sometime between August 1870 and the summer of the following year—when the engineers gave up on steam entirely—there was a contest to drill down from the top of mountain towards Lewis Tunnel. John William Henry and his hammer—maybe 9 pounds, or 12, maybe even 20—took on the Burleigh steam drill, and won.

John Henry has been seen as a hero by many different kinds of people. This illustration from 1936 by socialist Hugo Gellert shows John Henry as a strong, suffering working man. I believe images of muscled workers like this were an inspiration for drawings of Superman, which first appeared in the 1930s.

CHAPTER NINE

THE TRACKLINERS SPEAK

"Take this hammer"

I had found where and when a prisoner named John Henry probably died. Now, finally, I could go back to the questions that started me on my quest: Why did trackliners sing about this man, John Henry, and his hammer? Knowing who John Henry really was, I decided to listen to the trackliners' song again to try to find out what it was saying. Today most people sing John Henry as a song of strength and power. But when I listened carefully to the trackliners' John Henry songs, they sounded sad. They did not sound like a celebration of victory.

Why did John Henry die? It is easy to imagine that he somehow drove himself to a heart attack. But there is a much more likely possibility. Working in tunnels is dangerous, but because of tiny rocks, not large ones. Hammering on rock kicks up dust, and power drills are the worst. We know today that unless miners are careful, and unless the company takes precautions, workers in the mines breathe in a dust made up of the smallest fragments of rock. This mist causes various diseases including silicosis and pneumonicosis (also known as black lung) and has killed miners throughout the world. This deadly mixture can cause a lingering slow death over four or five years, or it can kill you right away. Anyone working side by side with a steam drill in a closed tunnel was doomed. The contest itself killed John Henry.

No. 1.

Diseases treated in the hospital of Virginia Peni
1871, to September 30th.

DISEASES.	Cases.
Amputations,	1
Consumption,	17
Cataract,	1
Diarrhœa, chronic.	5
Dropsy,	13
Epilepsy,	1
Enlargement of spleen,	1
Fractures,	1
Frost bite,	4
General debility and old age,	8
Gunshot and other wounds,	11
Hydropericardium,	1
Hernia,	2
Intermittent fever,	3
Jaundice.	2

This table from a report to the board of the Virginia State Penitentiary in 1872 shows illnesses treated by the prison surgeon. "Consumption" was the greatest cause of death in the penitentiary and the "consumption" that was killing the railroad workers was most likely silicosis, a lung disease similar to black lung.

No wonder the Board of the Virginia Penitentiary was called into action into 1872: Hundreds of prisoners were dying from breathing the dust in the Lewis Tunnel. That year one out of every ten men in the prison died. Working on the railroad was killing prisoners at a terrible rate.

Three hundred eighty black prisoners were working at the tunnels in 1872. When they hired the convicts, the C&O had promised to pay a large fine if the prisoner, or his body, did not come back at the end of the job—that way the railroad made sure none of them ran away. The C&O gathered the bodies of the men killed by the dust in Lewis Tunnel and sent them back to the penitentiary. The prison did not want anyone to know about all those deaths, so they dug holes and buried the 300 bodies in the sand.

John Henry simply vanishes from the prison record in 1873 as if he had disappeared into the air. The railroad and the prison wanted the story to end here—the tunnel was built on time, Huntington won his bet, the prisoners were buried, no one was the wiser. But that is not what happened. Because not everyone died. Cal Evans was a cook who had worked at Lewis and had then come to Big Bend Tunnel in 1875. He kept telling everyone stories about John

Henry. And then there was a waterboy, whose name is lost to history, who knew over a hundred verses of songs about John Henry. Cal and the boy took the story from Lewis to Big Bend—where people started to sing it and pass it on.

The song told of the contest and the prison, but that was not all. When I went back to the sad words of one of the very first versions of the John Henry song that were ever written down, I was able to understand what the trackliners were saying:

This old hammer
Killed John Henry,
Killed my brother,
Can't kill me.

Take this hammer,
Hammer to the captain
Tell him I'm gone
Tell him I'm gone.

The trackliners were singing the song as a warning. They were not just singing about one man and one hammer. They were telling other black men about what happened to prisoners, about men who worked in the tunnels and were buried in the sand. They were saying, run away, stay away, be aware, know the stories people try to hide. The 40,000 black men across the South were message-bearers, sending out the news to any who knew how to listen.

    I finally had the full story, not only the record of one man who most probably was the John Henry in the song, but of what the song was saying. I finally heard the trackliners speak. History had tried to silence many black men, some in prisons, some in graves, some in jobs no one ever recorded. But those men did speak in a song that now we all sing. They spoke, and because of the postcard, and the buried bodies, and the big ledger, and the engineering reports, we all can listen. The trackliners were telling the world: The hammer that killed John Henry
    Can't kill me.

APPENDICES

THE SEARCH GOES ON

Who was John William Henry? Why was a young man from Elizabeth, New Jersey, in Richmond just after the Civil War? So far we only have hints and clues with no clear answers.

I checked the records of black soldiers who fought in the Civil War, and he was not listed there. Perhaps at just over five feet tall, he was too short to serve. Elizabeth was a town in which most of the people were poor. A teenager from Elizabeth might have heard that there was work in Richmond after the war and headed down there to seek his fortune.

State records in New Jersey list a Henry family living near Elizabeth in 1850, when John would have been three. A "(b)" next to the family indicates that they were black. But Silvester and Ellen are shown with three children, Frederic (6), Deborah (4), and Catherine (1), no John. John could have been born a year after Deborah and two before Catherine, but there is no evidence that he was. And there is one lead that points in another direction: The man who reported on John's trial called him a "freed boy." That implies he had been a slave until recently. Why would a teenager from New Jersey be a slave? Perhaps he was taken from New Jersey shortly after he was born and grew up in the South.

New Jersey was slow to abolish slavery and reluctant to do so. While a law passed in 1804 said any children born into slavery would eventually be free—at 21 for a girl, 25 for boy—slave owners found various ways around the rules. In fact slavery was not completely ended in the state until 1846, the year before John Henry was born. Might a slave owner have whisked a baby out of the state to avoid the law? Possibly—and birth records in the state only begin in May 1848, so once more we are close, but blocked.

A group of teenagers in Elizabeth, New Jersey, is looking to see if they can find more evidence in old church records. A church might have a record of when John was baptized. Were there other Henry families in the area? Can we find out more about Silvester and Ellen? Perhaps some missing army record will identify the John Henry in the photograph from City Point (see page 42), and we can see if his middle name was William. Maybe the teenagers will find out more about John Henry, or maybe you will. Any reader whose family name was Henry around the time of the Civil War should check family stories you've heard and any records you can find to see if they link up with what we know of John William.

MANY JOHN HENRYS:

Versions of the Songs

My research began with the trackliners. I studied "John Henry" in order to learn about them. But that is not the only story the song has to tell. When I began my research, other scholars had already learned how the song changed after Cal Evans brought it to Big Bend. Three very different groups of people began to sing it, each in its own way: black prisoners, white miners, and black trackliners.

One of the very first descriptions of someone singing "John Henry" was written in 1915. William Aspinwall Bradley heard a prisoner named "Bad Bill" sing a popular song called "John Henry," or "The Steam Drill." Prisoners were kept away from their families, so it is not surprising that their versions were often about Polly Ann—the woman John left behind.

> *John Henry had a little wife,*
> *And the dress she wore was red;*
> *The last thing before he died,*
> *He said, "Be true to me when I'm dead,*
> *Oh, be true to me when I'm dead.*

TRACKLINERS, BLUES & ROCK AND ROLL

Where did the music called "the blues" come from? What is the origin of the term "rock and roll"? Historians and music scholars have had many debates on these questions. I think both can be traced to the trackliners and the men blasting tunnels for the southern railroads. The South from the 1870s was a place where tens of thousands of African-American men experimented with words, songs, and musical styles, as indicated in this photograph from 1902.

Trackliner songs left a break for the moment when the team needed to dog the track together. I think these songs with space for breaks are the origin of the blues. For example a trackliner song that went

Now I got a gal [huh] works in the yard
She brings me meat [huh] she brings me lard

Became the blues song, "Drop that Sack":

I got a girl [pause]
She works in the yard [pause]
She brings me meat [pause]
She brings me lard [pause].

Between the whacks of a hammer, shakers would either "rock" or "roll" the drill. I believe that is where the phrase "rock and roll" comes from. Miners were singing about what they were actually doing. But the first recorded use of the words "rock and roll" is in a blues song from

> the 1920s, well after the tunnels were built. By then rock and roll no longer had to do with mining. It was from this blues phrase that, in the 1940s and '50s, the idea of rock-and-roll music was born.

When white coal miners sang "John Henry," they combined it with their old Welsh and Scottish songs. For example, one verse in a miner's version of "John Henry" went,

Darlin' who gonna buy your slippers (yes)
Well-a who gonna glove your hand (yah, yah)
Say now who gonna kiss your rosy cheeks
Darlin' who gonna be your man (oh, lord)
Well-a who gonna be your man.

Those words were taken directly from a four-hundred-year old ballad called "The Lass of Loch Royal":

Oh, who will shoe your pretty little feet?
Who will glove your hand?

*And who will kiss your sweet little lips,
While I'm in a foreign land?*

And when trackliners were no longer spreading the word about the Lewis Tunnel, they used the song to talk about their own work:

*I can ball a jack
I can line a track
I can pick and shovel too.*

To "ball a jack" means to work as hard as a machine.

These three versions were just the start. "John Henry" became a song about strong black men. Henry has appeared on postage stamps, in children's books, in novels. His song has been recorded endlessly, and probably right now some school group or summer camp gathering is singing out the story of the steel-driving man.

"John Henry" has become an American song, and every group that sings it leaves traces in the lines and verses they add. But at first it was a message about one death trap of a tunnel. And that is a message we can now finally hear.

MAP OF THE CHESAPEAKE & OHIO RAILROAD IN 1873

This map shows the route taken by the C&O through the Lewis and Big Bend tunnels. From Charleston (in present-day West Virginia), train lines eventually reached Cincinnati, Chicago, and points west.

Laying track through the Appalachians was a formidable challenge for railroad engineers.

HOW TO BE A HISTORIAN
BY MARC ARONSON

Scott Nelson's search for the real John Henry is a model of what all historians do. There are six stages to his work.

1. Finding what is known already

A historian's first step is to find out what other researchers have already discovered. This saves him (or her) from repeating work that has already been done and from falling into mistakes or errors that have already been caught. For example, older history books used to say that Reconstruction was a mistake. Immature blacks and greedy northern "carpetbaggers," these books claimed, were ruining the South. But ever since Eric Foner carefully studied Reconstruction, we have learned these were largely myths spread by southern whites eager to regain control.

2. Checking their sources

An encyclopedia, a textbook, a Web site, or a biography will have plenty of information. But the authors did not get their facts and insights from the sky. In fact, these are called "secondary sources" because the authors are giving you their own judgments, as opposed to original, or "primary," sources. For example, a book of primary sources on "John Henry" would be just the songs, interviews with people who sang it, and documents, such as the names on the big ledger. A secondary source, such as this book, reviews those original materials and selects and interprets them. That makes it easier for the reader but also means the author has introduced his or her own conclusions. Any good source will give you a roadmap to further research—that may be in the form of citations and source notes in a bibliography or a list of further readings. Gather as many primary and secondary sources as you can and compare them. Following that trail offers many rewards.

3. Finding gaps and disagreements and formulating your own questions

As you see how a story has been passed from one book to another, you are likely to begin to see gaps, subjects that have not been covered, questions that have not been asked or answered. You may also run into contradictions, places where sources disagree. For example, Scott read in other histories that John Henry died at Big Bend, which meant that he could not have worked with C.R. Mason. And yet there was a report that Mason had been John Henry's supervisor. How could that be? The contradiction between the two reports told Scott that something was not right.

4. Looking for new evidence

Scott went to Big Bend, where he learned that no steam drills could have been used in making the tunnel. That new evidence helped him to solve the mystery of John Henry. Even if you cannot take a field trip to a historical site, you can think of new kinds of evidence. For example, Scott wanted to know about the trackliners, but they were hardly mentioned in history books. He needed to think about how he could learn more about people who left no writing and were not interviewed by reporters or studied by scholars. He realized that workers sing songs and that their songs might help us to understand their lives.

Historians use many kinds of evidence to learn more about the past. For example, until very recently women could not vote, and so they hardly appeared in political histories. How could we know more about their opinions? Some scholars noticed that women read and wrote a great deal in the 1800s, so they have studied letters, diaries, even popular novels, to learn more about women and their beliefs. Similarly, other scholars have looked at the words young people sing when playing double Dutch, or hopscotch, even jokes or insults. All of those have histories that can be traced and will help us to know more about how young people lived in the past.

5. Expanding the search

Scott was stumped when he could not find the engineers' reports, which were said to have been destroyed. By expanding his search to include any of the men who were said to have worked with John Henry or other prisoners, he eventually did find the reports. Historians know that records from the past are not always neatly labeled in ways that make them easy to find. If they were, very likely someone would have already studied them. So while there are no official New Jersey records for births in 1847, there may be records kept by churches in which babies were baptized. If you are stuck, ask a librarian for other ways to frame your search.

6. Sharing what you have found

Showing your research to classmates, teachers, or parents is very useful. A historian needs insights from others, especially when looking at new evidence or coming up with new theories. After all, just because an idea is new does not mean it is true. While Scott was doing his research, he showed drafts to other historians who were especially knowledgeable about southern history. This gave him the assurance that he had not missed a key fact or ignored an important piece of evidence.

SUGGESTIONS FOR FURTHER READING

NONFICTION: HISTORY

Rhoda Blumberg, *Full Steam Ahead: The Race to Build a Transcontinental Railroad* (Washington, D.C.: National Geographic Society, 1996).

> Filled with large illustrations, this tells the story of the Union Pacific and the Central Pacific Railroad companies.

Mary Ann Fraser, *Ten Mile Day and the Building of the Transcontinental Railroad* (New York: Henry Holt, 1996).

> A full-color picture book for older readers with accurate, detailed illustrations showing how the Irish and Chinese workers laid track in the West on the way to the Golden Spike ceremony.

Joy Hakim, *A History of US: Book Seven: Reconstructing America 1865-1890* (New York: Oxford University Press, 2003).

Written in a lively, engaging style, this is a survey of U.S. history in John Henry's times.

Monica Halpern, *Railroad Fever: Building the Transcontinental Railroad 1830-1870* (Washington, D.C.: National Geographic Society, 2003).

A good choice if you want a brief, photo-filled overview of the story of the railroads. You might start your research here before going on to longer books.

Milton Meltzer, *Hear That Train Whistle Blow! How the Railroad Changed the World* (New York: Random House, 2004).

Well written and readable, the book includes two pages on John Henry and conditions for workers like him.

Liza Tuttle, *A Multicultural Portrait of the Railroads* (New York: Benchmark Books, 1994).

While this book only has two short paragraphs on John Henry, the multicultural view of American history it offers is valuable.

THE SONG

Amy L. Cohn (editor), *From Sea to Shining Sea: A Treasury of American Folklore and Folk Songs* (New York: Scholastic, 1993).

>Illustrated by 11 Caldecott medal and four Caldecott honor book artists, this is a wonderful anthology of stories, songs, and verse that covers themes in American history. The section that includes the song "John Henry" (eight verses plus music) has a short piece called *Building the Transcontinental Railroad.*

Kathleen Krull (editor), *Gonna Sing My Head Off! American Folk Songs for Children* (New York: Alfred A. Knopf, 1992).

>Primarily a songbook with music, this book includes the song—nine verses plus the music—as well as

a short paragraph about John Henry.

THE FOLKTALE

Ezra Jack Keats, *John Henry: An American Legend* (New York: Dragonfly Books, 1987).

> A classic retelling of the folktale by a Caldecott Medal winner.

Brad Kessler (author) and Barry Jackson (illustrator), *John Henry: The Legendary Folk Hero* (New York: Rabbit Ears Books, 2000).

> This version includes an audio cassette, narrated by Denzel Washington.

Julius Lester (author) and Jerry Pinkney (illustrator), *John Henry* (New York: Dial Books, 1994).

> A beautiful version—both pictures and text have a rhythm and energy that brings the story to life.

FOLKTALE COLLECTIONS

Mary Pope Osborne (author) and Michael McCurdy (illustrator), *American Tall Tales* (New York: Alfred A. Knopf, 1991).

> The version of John Henry's story in this collection begins with his birth. The writing is strong and vivid and includes "Notes on the Story."

Paul Robert Walker (author) and James Bernardin (illustrator), *Big Men, Big Country: A Collection of American Tall Tales* (San Diego: Harcourt Brace Jovanovich, 1993).

> The version of the John Henry story retold here only covers the Big Bend Tunnel race. It includes a note on the "true" story.

WHERE TO HEAR THE SONGS

A good place to hear historic recordings of some of the versions of the song and learn more about John Henry is this Web site created by four graduate students at the University of North Carolina at Chapel Hill:

> http://www.ibiblio.org/john_henry/songlist.html

This John Henry site hosted by National Public Radio contains song recordings and useful links to other John Henry resources on the Internet:

> http://www.npr.org/programs/morning/features/patc/johnhenry/

Two versions of "John Henry" and 10 railroad work songs form a very small part of the nearly 700 sound recordings of The John and Ruby Lomax 1939 Southern States Recording Trip. These historic recordings can be sampled online through the Library of Congress at

> http://memory.loc.gov/ammem/lohtml/

A NOTE ABOUT MY SOURCES

BY SCOTT REYNOLDS NELSON

When I began studying John Henry, I started with the work of Guy Johnson. Johnson was a college professor at the University of North Carolina in the 1920s, and he marveled at the songs that black construction workers sang as they dug trenches and built buildings on the UNC campus. He even heard some of these songs outside the window of his office. With another professor in 1926 he wrote *Negro Workaday Songs* in which both professors wrote down and analyzed black workers' songs. Johnson was a sociology professor and so was interested in what work songs said about workers' daily lives. Johnson devoted a whole chapter of *Negro Workaday Songs* to "John Henry" and was struck by how this song seemed to describe an actual event. Johnson then sent out a request to students in black high schools and colleges, promising a reward for the best version of the "John Henry" song they could find. He asked contestants to write down the song and describe how they first heard it. He then used these contest entries as his sources, and he was struck by the reoccurrence of the C&O railroad in many of the "John Henry" songs he received. Maybe this was a real person, he thought. He then wrote to officers on the railroad for further information and took some of his students on a trip to Talcott, West Virginia, to interview black and white people about the songs.

Unfortunately for Johnson, another professor, Lewis Chappell, was also working on the topic of the "John Henry" song, and Chappell lived closer to Talcott, West Virginia. Chappell visited the area around 1927 or so, about a year before Johnson got there. Chappell didn't like black people very much and insulted some of the black men whom he asked about the John Henry song. Chappell called one black man a "damn liar," which was a very mean insult in those days. Chappell only trusted what white people told him about the song. By the time that Johnson and his students arrived in Talcott, most black people refused to talk to them. They kept the story to themselves.

Johnson wrote a book called *John Henry: Tracking Down a Negro Legend.* It showed how he had done his work and whom he had interviewed. A few years later Chappell published his own book called *John Henry: A Folk-Lore Study.*

In 2005 I wrote an article with long footnotes describing my discovery of the John Henry materials. The article is called "Who Was John Henry? Railroad Construction, Southern Folklore and the Birth of Rock and Roll." It was published in a journal called *Labor: Studies of Working Class History of the Americas.* I then published a book called *Steel Drivin' Man: John Henry, the Untold Story of an American Legend* for Oxford University Press in 2006. Any teacher or motivated student who wants to know more about my sources can find them in the article or book.

BACK COVER MATERIAL

The Civil War was just over, and all across the South, African-American men were building the railroads. The songs they sang tell their stories, if you only know how to listen.

***

Join Scott Reynolds Nelson as he follows the song "John Henry" until we can hear those voices loud and clear.

Scott Reynolds Nelson is the Legum Professor of History at the College of William & Mary. *Steel Drivin' Man: John Henry: The Untold Story of an American Legend,* his adult book on the search for John Henry, has earned many honors including the Merle Curti Award by the Organization of American Historians as the best history book of 2006, the Anisfield-Wolf award for contributions to our understanding of race and racism, and the National

Award for Arts Writing. Nelson notes, "I loved John Henry as a kid but hated history. I thought it was all about names and dates. I hope other kids will learn from this book that history is something you do, not just something you read." He lives with his wife and two children in Williamsburg, Virginia.

Marc Aronson is an award-winning author and editor who earned his doctorate in American History at NYU. He is the co-author of *The World Made New* for National Geographic, a new biography of Robert Kennedy, and *Race: A History Beyond Black and White.* He found the entire process of working on this book with Dr. Nelson a treat. Aronson lives with his wife and two sons in Maplewood, New Jersey.

Index

A
African Americans,
  chain gangs, *41, 42, 54, 58*
  in Civil War, *52, 54*
  railroad workers, *9, 10, 13, 16, 38, 74, 75*
  in Reconstruction, *56*
  in Virginia Penitentiary, *42, 44, 46, 49, 54, 74*
Allegheny Mountains, *2, 23, 29, 58*

B
Big Bend Mountain, *37*
Big Bend Tunnel, *24, 29, 34, 37, 64, 66, 74*
Burleigh, Charles, *29*
Burleigh steam drill, *29, 35, 68*

C
Central Pacific Railroad, *28*
Chain gangs, *41, 42, 54, 58*
Chesapeake & Ohio Railway, (see Covington and Ohio Railroad),
Chinese workers, *13, 26, 28*
City Point, Virginia, *52, 53*
Civil Rights movement, *56*
Civil War, African Americans in, *52, 54*
Covington and Ohio Railroad (Chesapeake and Ohio Railway, C&O), *22, 23, 24, 26, 35, 41, 42, 58, 62, 63, 66, 74*
Crocker, Charles, *28*

D
Daugherty, James, *2*
Davis, Jefferson, *56*
Dogging the track, *17, 18*
Drillers, *62*
Dynamite, *26, 29*

E
Emancipation Proclamation, *56*
Evans, Cal, *74*

G
Gellert, Hugo, *68, 71*
Golden Spike ceremony, *26, 28*
Grady, Henry, *16, 41, 42, 44*
Grant, Ulysses S., *52*
Great Bend Tunnel, (see Big Bend Tunnel),
  Hammer man, *62*

H
Harris, Leon R., *37*
Hayden, Palmer, *3*
Henry, John, (see also 'John Henry' song),
  arrest and trial of, *49, 53, 54*
  contest with steam drill, *5, 24, 34, 66, 68, 74, 75*
  Daugherty drawing of, *2*
  death of, *3, 41, 71*
  Gellert illustration of, *68, 71*
  Hayden painting of, *3*
  Long illustration of, *58, 62*
  Nelson's search for real man behind song and legend, *5, 8, 20, 22, 23, 34, 37, 38, 40, 41, 42, 44, 46, 47, 49, 53, 62, 63, 64, 66, 68, 71, 74, 75*
  photograph of, *49, 52*
  physical appearance of, *37*
  statue of, *34*

in Virginia Penitentiary, *41, 46, 47, 49, 54, 58*

Hopkins, Mark, *28*

Huntington, Collis Potter, *26, 28, 29, 34, 62*

I

Irish workers, *13, 28*

'John Henry' song, lyrics of, *5, 20, 22, 23, 24, 40, 44, 66, 75*

versions of, *18, 22, 23, 24*

L

Leschot's rotary diamond drill, *29*

Lewis Tunnel, *62, 63, 64, 66, 68, 74*

Lincoln, Abraham, *56*

Long, Frank W., *58, 62*

Lung diseases, *71, 74*

M

Making the grade, *5, 8*

Mason, C.R., *64*

Muckers, *62*

N

Nelson, Scott Reynolds,
childhood of, *8, 9, 10, 34*

postcard as clue for, *2, 5, 8, 38, 40, 63, 75*

search for real John Henry behind the song and legend, *5, 8, 20, 22, 23, 34, 37, 38, 40, 41, 42, 44, 46, 47, 49, 53, 62, 63, 64, 66, 68, 71, 74, 75*

study of railroads by, *10, 16, 26*

working style of, *8*

Nitroglycerine, *26*

P

Perry, A.H., *64*

Petersburg, Virginia, *52, 53*

Pneumonicosis (black lung), *71, 74*

Prince George County, Virginia, *49, 52, 53*
Promontory Point, Utah, *28*

R

Rail spike, *16, 22*
Reconstruction, *38, 56*
Richmond, Fredericksburg, & Potomac Railroad, *44*
'Ring around the Rosy', *16*
Rock and roll, *62*

S

Sanford, Florida, *9*
Shakers, *62*
Shanties, shantlings, *38*
Sierra Mountains, *26, 28*
Silberger, Manuel, *18, 20*
Silicosis, *71, 74*
Songs, (see also 'John Henry' song),

tracklining, *16, 18, 20, 71, 75*
Stanford, Leland, *28*
Steam drills, *26, 34, 35, 37, 62, 66, 68, 74*
 percussive, *29, 35*
 rotary diamond, *29, 35*
Superman, *71*

T

Tracklining, *13, 16, 20, 22*
Tracklining songs, *16, 18, 20, 71, 75*
Transcontinental Railroad, *28*

U

Union Army, *52*
Union Pacific Railroad, *23, 24, 28*

V

Virginia Penitentiary, Richmond, *38, 40, 41, 42, 44, 46, 47, 49, 54, 56, 58, 74*

W

Wages, *13, 42*
Walters, Tommy, *64*
Wardwell, Burnham, *56, 58*
Whitcomb, H.D., *64*
White house, *38, 40, 41, 44, 49, 63*
Wiseman's grocery store, *53, 54*
Work conditions, *16*

CPSIA information can be obtained
at www.ICGtesting.com
Printed in the USA
LVHW022025070222
710478LV00005B/389